LOVE N

WALTER RINDER

LOVE IS MY REASON

Text and photography by the author

CELESTIAL ARTS
Millbrae, California

Copyright © 1975 by Celestial Arts
231 Adrian Road, Millbrae, California 94030

First printing: August 1975
Second printing: September 1975
Made in the United States of America

Library of Congress Cataloging in Publication Data

Rinder, Walter.
    Love is my reason.

    I. Title.
PS3568.I5L65   818'.5'4   75-9444
ISBN 0-89087-105-1

DEDICATION

To Don Labbe

A better friend a man could not have

INTRODUCTION

At the moment, I live in the shadow of a great white mountain. I have had the opportunity to spend many quiet hours wrapped in solitude within the peacefulness of the forest. When night approaches, the darkness brings with it contemplation. Often I walk down to the river and gaze about, feeling the nature of life flowing through me. Always my eyes come to rest on the star-filled sky, in wonderment. My mind wanders through the heavens, darting from one star to another, finding man's symbols of the Little and Big Dipper and the Milky Way. What mysteries, what secrets are out there that would give me greater understanding, slow but a little my restless spirit? Intently I look for a sign, an omen, that might reveal a truth as yet unknown to me. My mind flashes to memories. People's faces then replace the stars and the darkness between becomes places where I planted roots, for awhile.

Fantasy and dreams become my master, overtaking my reality. My spirit, stripped of intense conflicts, releases suppression from my mind; my then naked thoughts touched by the elements which filter from beyond the earth, whispering . . . (as if a million morning glories are opening their petals to the warmth of the sun) . . . "There is a better way, there is a better way." Where you find loneliness, share togetherness; where you find pain, share relief; where you find non-caring, share a reason to care. Where you find desolation, share in the rebuilding; where you find hope lying barren, share in the cultivation of trust. There is a better way. Life is precious and do not abandon the little time you are allowed to let the world know of you.

Listen to the whispering.

A PERSONAL STATEMENT

I have written this book, these personal statements, very spontaneously, allowing my feelings to flow through my pen in the words you read. I have not followed a prescribed path or tried to achieve social acceptance either with my concepts or the placement of the photographs in this book. I did not care to create a balance or harmony to the entire book, only with each individual page. Each person reading it will find individual continuity, personal harmony.

Thoughts are duplicated, but in reading it over I find repetition helpful in seeking to simplify the complicated, in giving understanding that might have been missed. I use some words many times because those particular words have important meaning to me.

Sometimes I feel the adult intellect. Other times I write with the simplicity of a child. There are moments that my words seem inadequate to describe the depth of my feelings, and rereading causes me frustration because I am concerned my words may be misinterpreted or misunderstood.

My Gemini nature: ever changing, ever questioning, fascinated by all thought and logic. Traveling time and space on the wings of love.

My photography is as important to me as my writing in sharing my life with you. All the people and places you see have been or are an integral part of my life.

Please feel free to write me of your feelings, your comments on what I have to say in this book. We all need ways to express ourselves. Through the expression of others, we can learn about ourselves.

Walter Rinder c/o: Celestial Arts
231 Adrian Road, Millbrae, California 94030

LOVE IS MY REASON

A flourescent orange sun hid itself behind the tall cluster
of evergreen which rose high above the bank of the Sandy
River. The man had watched many suns set and rise in
his life. This day's sun had been the herald of a special
enlightenment which would follow the man the rest of his
life. "Live your feelings." Today he had made a decision,
to change his way of life, his surroundings. He was
moving back into the city. Not the same one he had left
when he built his house in the mountains, but one many
thousands of miles away.

The man realized that his main responsibility was to himself. From that realization he gained personal strength and self confidence and understood the weakness in himself. This weakness could only be overcome by his own motivation to venture into new levels of awareness. He had never married nor felt the need to bring children into the world. There were far too many kids already on this earth who needed love and someone to care about them. Why add to the burden? He would share his life with those who were alone—with those who needed him.

He had never felt the need to be attached only to one person; loving many people had fulfilled his wants and needs, at least for periods of time or until the next encounter of intimacy and involvement.

A flock of mallard ducks, following the path of the river, flew past where he sat and the man again considered the unity of their flight. They destroyed nothing as they passed. How magnificent this natural world he had the chance to discover. The many species of plants and living things, the variety of their differences seemed to him perfection. They blended! Is civilization man's answer to truth? Each man must decide the question for himself. (There are both truth and fallacy inherent in civilization. People's interpretations disturbed the man.)

Even the deer had fled man's guns and traps. They could be seen only *occasionally* in the valley where once they had roamed in quantity as did the bear and beaver. Every living animal was precious to him. The chipmunks had built their home in the roof of his porch and he watched the family grow from two to five. Every once in a while he would look up to see their little faces peeking through the knot holes in the wood. A mother frog who had been with him when his house was first being built had found her mate. A year later—early in the morning—he saw on a large rock near his river four little frogs hopping about.

He gave almost two years of his life to the mountain, but in time his footprints would be effaced by those who came after. There were many small pieces of himself left on the soil: flowering bushes he had planted, a firepit down by the river, an old wagon wheel leaning against a dead stump (he had found it in a barn in Pennsylvania—it bore scars of the fire and carnage of the Civil War) and, most important, a house that others would make their home.

He laid foundations in life, started some building and completed some ideas. He was an instigator of creative thought, an artist painting beautiful pictures upon the dark walls of the mind. His dreams, his reality, his truth could not be taught by formal education, or religious institution, they could only be learned through actual experience. He'd go back into the mainstream of life, allowing life to penetrate the conformity he still held onto, resolve the conflicts that brought cold and hunger to his inner isolation. His heart yearned for peace but he realized that peace had to be fought for every day—it was never permanent.

To him, imagination was far more important than knowledge. Imagination created all types of artists (architects of truth and beauty) roaming the entire spectrum of thought, free as the wind. In the years of formal education, including several of college, he was taught to memorize certain facts, believe certain forms of behavior correct, accept the teachings of the educators as truth without question. He was pumped up with knowledge, filled to capacity with institutionalized learning, yet how much of it could he use in living his life! Where, in all those years was there any learning about the qualities of love, about togetherness, about the senses; a developing of the child's and youth's imagination, promoting their being different as being beautiful! How many years had it taken for the man to reprogram, to decondition, to tear down his memory bank of conventional concepts, to step beyond the boundary that separated *his* truth from *traditional* truth?

The man didn't want to hunt with a gun—neither his fellow man nor any other living creature. He didn't want to use his mind as a destructive weapon! He hunted with his camera, wanting to capture a feeling—not destroy a life form.

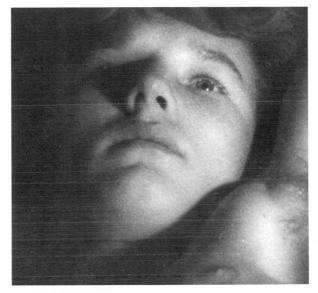

He made war upon the traditions of civilization, on the thinking and the premises on which these foundations were built, not with a destructive force but with a change of attitude.

Geese and a few cranes flew the river corridor in front of his home. There weren't many birds left. A few hummingbirds made their homes next to his, as did the woodpecker. He often put out nuts and pieces of bread and scraps of meat to attract the wild creatures. How excited he had been the day he saw a fox run across the highway not far from his home—they were all but extinct in the area!

All of his possessions were in his home. The antiques he had collected over the last couple of years were being saved for a time when they could once again be used, according to their function, on the land he hoped to acquire. Land on which a community of people could live close to the heartbeat of the earth, with a new way. Love as their reason. This was the greatest of all his dreams. The man had a vast array of handcrafted furniture, and many utensils that he and his friends had made.

Books by the hundreds filled his shelves. He found a few isolated minds which, for him, carried a great wealth of truth and inspiration—signposts that could help him on his journey into the unknown reaches of the mind—the unexplored depths of the soul.

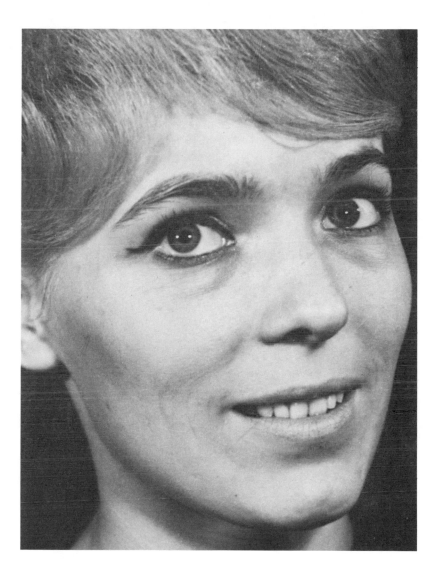

His photography adorned almost every wall of his house, reminding him of lessons learned, persons loved, places admired; windows of his life.

Those who found his home also found the windows never covered. He had no reason to hide from the sun by day, the moon by night, or from his feelings.

It was a simple two-level round house which blended with his environment. Nature filtered through the big picture windows facing the alder, the maple, the cedar, and the river. He could sit in his living room and watch the river current carry pieces of wood and leaves past his home on their journey to the ocean if they didn't get caught somewhere along the banks. The house was built mostly of wood and smelled of cedar. On windy nights he would lie in his bed listening to the creaking of the boards still settling themselves into the harmony of a strong structure. He had observed every part of his house being built and remembered the day of completion. His pride and satisfaction had made him very happy. He had all the comforts he wanted, feeling it was a tiny paradise upon the earth.

He contemplated the many years that had passed since he left home as a young explorer. An innocent to the outside world, knowing only that he was filled to capacity from the continual love of his parents and friends who had shared his childhood and youth. His purpose was to make love to the world as he encountered it and its people. He had not been schooled in a trade or profession, had no special skills or hobbies, though he had attended a local college. His only desire was to become involved with new places—to become intimate with people.

The unknown had become the center of his dreams. He thought he wanted to become a lover, a companion to all the beautiful people he felt his society was full of. He'd developed a romantic nature during his youth and his idealism was the vehicle for his mind, as he ventured into a much larger world than he had ever known before.

The seasons changed quickly and the pages of his books of memories grew thicker. Volumes were filled with recollections of tall buildings and country stores, hotel rooms and coffeehouses, risks and chances, relationships, love affairs that staggered the imagination as he remembered how easy it was for him to fall in love with a beautiful face or a gesture of sensitivity—a lonely voice or a plea for help. He was attracted to people for the beauty they held, never for their possessions, and he hoped his love would free that beauty.

To him it seemed if death came now he would have no regrets, for he had lived many lifetimes in his short span of years. Scattered over a wide area he had touched many life cycles, escaped many precarious situations, was deceived by many false motives. Growing in the joy of love, he left his heart with many.

All life was bearable. All life held intrigue, secrets yet to be uncovered. He had become very flexible to the harsh world called civilization. There were no longer any expectations, no absolutes, for these had confused his mind with endless hurts and anxieties.

The world he'd found was not what his boyish innocence had imagined. Much of his love had been challenged. He competed for relationships—his competitor often being money or physical beauty or social status or drugs. There were times when he was the prey, and others the predator. There seemed to be little time for courting and one night of love was the most many people would afford.

He found love rushed, cluttered into tiny moments, people being obsessed that tomorrow would never come. And sometimes, no matter the time element, love never came, never opened the door of his longing. So in and out of lives he came and went, and with each involvement he gained a little more insight into people, into himself.

His mountain home had given him the chance to put all the scattered pieces of his life together. The picture that emerged was again the knowledge of his true nature. His destiny was once more reclaimed.

No longer was he the tender, naive young man who left home with one suitcase, thirty-five dollars in his pocket and a one-way train ticket to Phoenix, Arizona, his first stop as he began to explore the world of his society.

He was now well-seasoned in his quest, in seeking new horizons which had led him on the path of writing. But he had never aspired to become an author. Man's lack of responding to his affection, to his simple warm nature, caused him to write his feelings during the many lonely hours when the objects of his feelings betrayed the openness of his emotions.

His intellect began to express what his body was not allowed by others to express. At times he wrote with tears, in silent compassion of the restraint his body had endured. At other times he wrote with the joy he felt when people loved and respected his expression of love. His writing increased, it grew and grew! The fulfillment of each poem ended as a written summation of an open, free relationship, of an involvement stifled by oppression. The torture of seeing people suffer from their own fears, and his own inner sufferings brought on by the conventional concepts of a society teaching *right* or *wrong* made boundaries for his love.

He spoke in silence with photos and poetry, hoping people would find him and become stimulated to escape from the traditions which bound them to unhappiness and loneliness and conflicts of emotions secretly hidden behind false images.

He had realized long ago that words by themselves didn't mean much. So he waited patiently for the actions behind those beautifully spoken words—actions which too often did not come. He found that many people lived by words alone, people who did not stimulate or motivate the art of building relationships.

Each year he grew a little more tired when he smiled or reached out to touch. The honest emotions of his personality had been badly mutilated. Somehow he always seemed to mend, continuing his journey of understanding and loving. His feelings were the precious gift given to him by his Creator, and life was the place he intended to project them.

God	Man
gives	gives
birth	birth
to	to
feelings	thoughts

It was during the times when he was alone that the thoughts of leaving the security of his home germinated in his mind. He had been there long enough. There were many more ways of life to live in his quest for understanding. His route would again take him back to the cities. He needed to share more of himself with the centers of change and culture—become more involved. But there was also a fear and an excitement about leaving the security and comforts of his friendly world. It was a safe world, protecting him from a much larger hostile world. There were no risks or chances to take because he had built it that way—to find a measure of peace.

Now the time had approached for him to again face life's turmoil, its pain and its struggle, with which he was all too familiar. He once more wished to become a part of his fellow man's struggle. The cities with their many kinds of humanity showed him he was a part of each, though in differing degrees. He realized he had many parts that had to manifest themselves if he was to feel comfortable with himself. The time spent in his mountain home had developed new parts, reinforced some old ones, and changed some familiar ones.

On this particular day he had realized that he still had not found that special place where he could build his dreams—a place where he belonged for more than just portions of his life.

He did not necessarily want to follow the highways of other men's minds or the ways of life of others, for the world was full of beaten paths. He wanted to journey wherever his inclinations took him, to create his own byways. Tradition had built the roadways of the world and while traveling them he could see the remnants of countless wars, the litter and material waste, and the wasted minds. He saw the destruction, the indifference, and the monuments man had built to his image. He saw people starved for affection, men killing other men because they would not accept one another.

He saw the crosses that bore dead men's flesh after the
hearts had been crushed and souls released—akin to the
Appian Way of Roman times, where crosses of wood
lined the edge of the road for miles. Men crucified
because they spoke out against tradition and did not
cower under slavery—men whose only crime was that
they would not accept the station in life dictated by
society. They could not give in to the tyrants. . . . men
who proclaimed themselves gods or who commanded
others as the generals of God.

Small trout and steelhead creased the surface of the water as the man watched the flowing current. He had become used to the river's sound. When the river was swollen from winter and spring rains, the loudness of her voice spoke to the man of her destiny and the life she gave to those living things that touched her. She wound herself around bends, through small gorges, and across grassy lands until she became a part of the mighty Columbia River, her waters becoming obscured. She played an important role, from her birth at the glacier on Mt. Hood to the end of her journey where she emptied into the greater river. She spoke to the man of the paradox of their lives. From his birth till his death he would affect all life with which he came in contact. She talked of the man's being so *fortunate* because he could experience and touch so much more of life than could she because he had more freedom of movement. She was confined to her banks. "We here have taught you all we are able—all you can now assimilate. Be not like the iceberg which shows only a small part of itself. Be like the mighty mountain so your wholeness can be seen from the plain by your people. "Go!," she urged.

The man had deep life lines about his eyes showing he had lived with struggle, but the eyes themselves were young and radiated excitement as though he had found the fountain of youth.

The man had never found a permanent peace, but had each day to renew it again. He had to rediscover constantly those precious moments when struggle ceased and tranquility prevailed. The moments he treasured most, those offering his soul its greatest release, were when he made love.

Darkness came over the land, but within the man's heart the sun continued to shine and many people were to be touched by the warmth of that sun in the years to come.

TWO

THE ACTOR WE ARE

I personally feel I would rather be alone than play peoples' games of love. You see, I'm not a very good game player and I never really learned the rules. I guess you've got to like yourself so the times you are alone you still keep growing, building your life and not just sitting in the armchair of pity, feeling sorry for yourself. After awhile the old armchair begins to feel uncomfortable.

I've been alone many times in my life. When I was younger I'd run out into the streets in search of someone with whom to share. After awhile I got tired of collecting memory moments. It was hard then for a young idealist to play the many games, with their differing rules, each made by a different person. After years in the game factory, I discovered that my time alone allowed me the freedom to be totally myself, spontaneous and without restrictions. Time spent alone isn't easy but caring about yourself sure helps.

If I am restricted by people's limitations in the exploration of their minds, bodies and spirits, then those times I elect to spend alone give me the opportunity to read books, which may be vicarious living but nevertheless I still pursue my dream of learning about life and about myself. Books should not be an escape that one depends on as a substitute for living. They should spark the reader's curiosity and imagination, and they should encourage his capacity to seek new ways of expression.

When I am alone I play my guitar, though I have not yet mastered it. I find pleasure in singing and in playing my own music, thinking as I do of people I have known. I often work in my photographic darkroom, creating photos for no other purpose than my own enjoyment. And often I drive to the downtown section of the city when I am alone. At night, on the streets, I meet the most interesting people, sharing conversation and an intimacy that I could seldom find among my friends. The night people are truly actors, playing their roles with fervent determination and in earnest. They are very spontaneous and seem to act more by instinct for survival than do the day people who wear the masks of convention and uniformity and whose acts are very predictable.

I am writing quite a bit more now, for even in our loneliness we need to share—with the kitchen stove, words on a page, pictures in a magazine, our home, an old snapshot album, our plants. Music helps—it creates moods, brings back memories touring the attics of our minds.

I would rather be alone than pretend at love or a relationship. When I first enter a person's life he is suspicious of my motives, and only time and patience will overcome the fear and distrust. Sometimes my love becomes tired of the struggle, and I withdraw to myself, saying goodbye.

There are two ingredients I have found in human behavior that create the most distrust: the essence of love and being different; yet they are the most honest.

The magic of love. Oh how I wish the world were full of magicians—as it is full of Dreams.

An actor am I and I wear a mask. I wear many masks at different times. I play many roles upon the stage of life. All the parts I play are me while I am acting a particular role. Each time I wear a mask you see one of those roles. Very few people have stayed around long enough to experience many of my parts. The actor is my soul, the core of my true nature. The masks I wear or the parts I play are the manifestations of that soul; that of the writer, the photographer, the traveler, the explorer, the philosopher, the orator, the builder, the musician, the collector of old things, the historian, the court jester, the extrovert, the introvert, the humanitarian, the loner, the idealist, the dreamer. Each is a mask revealing only one part of the whole. Some of the roles I play are more important, are more dramatic, have a greater impact upon life. The years will teach me more that I am not aware of if I am open to learning.

So even when you are alone the play of life continues and you exchange masks, only, you are the audience.

There are few true artists among us, though most of us dabble at art. The latter quite often are the game players. True artists are committed and devoted, their art being their first, most important love.

The original truth for artists is to extend themselves in their art, sharing with their fellowman what they interpret to be their true beliefs and feelings, disclosing themselves. When alone, or in our times of loneliness, we can practice the actor we are.

As the curtain of life opens once again, step onto the stage of your existence wearing a new mask, playing a new part, expanding your talents. Play your parts well, my friends, with all the realism and drama of which you are capable. The parts in the play you are portraying were written by our Creator. What a magnificent playwright!

EPILOGUE

Being alone or loneliness is only one mask that we wear. Let the actor you are play whatever parts you wish to explore. There are so many. If you find after performing a role you are not comfortable in that part you have free choice to change at any time.

The curtain slowly opens. The orchestra starts the overture. You are given your cue. The audience is patiently awaiting your entrance upon the stage of life. What role will you play? No one else can play your parts.

THREE

LOVE IS WORTH LIVING

My being in love with love and my intimacy with our earth motivates my speaking to everyone I meet quite freely and uninhibitedly and without payment. I ask nothing in return but the courtesy, and the curiosity of yourselves to be attentive, listening to my thoughts. My feelings are open to your criticism, to your debate, to your acknowledgement and to your self-identity. You may probe my soul, suckle my thoughts, have me for your confidant, your information bureau. You may use me for your needs as long as we can grow together, as long as we learn from one another and our intentions are the rebirth of human dignity.

We are born twice, once in our bodies and again in our minds. The second birth is when the human being realizes the individual that lies within the body.

Man's greatest struggle which leads to man's greatest reward is finding ways to express his individuality. But you will never know this unless you become involved, not with trite, meaningless things just to get through the day. Not by attaching yourself to the fun seekers, for they abuse time; or the money seekers, for their folly is the absence of love. Not with false communication which destroys the bridges of the soul. Not by becoming attached to the normal man for collectively he consumes the most from life and produces the least, creating imbalance.

First become involved with yourself. Then start exploring, for the world of the body and of the mind is enormous. You may not discover gold or riches but you should find the individual that is you. The world of the mind is endless. We've mapped so little of the mind! I sometimes feel that is why one fears the unknown territory beyond his tiny world which is already over-crowded, cluttered by habits and decayed with old ideas. There are ways of life beyond the known world that would amaze you. People, out there, are living them.

There are human beings who have found a vehicle with which to travel and who are looking for others who also wish to explore. If you can't find your own vehicle, join them. They feel love is worth living. They feel "if you're not part of the solution then you're part of the problem." They are the pioneers of *now* who have dedicated themselves to the journey of finding a true purpose and reason. They do not want to become carbon-copy men. Find a vehicle and join them. If you don't have one of your own they will help you to build one, for they care. Believe me. I know. I have been on a lot of expeditions.

Many people feel material possessions such as a motor
cycle, a car, a stereo, a T.V., any of the riches of
technology, will solve their problems or fulfill their needs
in finding a purpose or seeking a reason in justifying
their existence. The vehicles chosen are only as good as
the reason for having them. Too many vehicles go in
circles, leading nowhere. These vehicles can help carry us
to new worlds if we will take them away from habit and
conformity. We'll meet many travelers and outcasts
along the way for the roads of our society are filled with
the rejects who will not follow the herd, wandering from
concept to concept, from experience to experience. Their
individual involvements in exploring can influence the
giant mold that our society has created. They are seeking
their own truths, and their deeds, projected in many
ways, create conflict and change within the structured
way of life of the parent society.

If a woman and I choose to live together as a family, love being our reason, without a formal declaration of marriage, it is interpreted by some standards as sinful; yet God calls it love. Society would condemn me as a pervert if I fall in love with a person of my own sex; yet God calls it love. I am useless, a bum, a reject, if I do not hold a steady job or at least exhibit a willingness to work and hold to their standards of success. I am insane or mentally disturbed if I do not fit into society's category of normal behavior and then they would try to modify my feelings, reprogram my actions. My body must be imprisoned, or I must pay retribution, if I do not obey laws which I consider unjust, because then I am a menace to the sanctuary of their ideology. Under all circumstances where society labors or plays, I must cover parts of my body because society feels God's creation is indecently exposed.

I can no longer accept many of the social pressures that are contrary to my nature though I would not maliciously hurt any individual or cause any act that would suppress another's freedom. There is a balance to conformity as well as to nonconformity. My conscience searches out that balance.

I shall never abandon my feelings or their manifestations. I shall never abandon my affair with life or the intimacy that one-to-one relationships can create sensually and sexually and spiritually. I shall never cease speaking my mind, even in the face of intimidation, condemnation, imprisonment or death. Never could I renounce what I know love to be and the elation I feel when it is lived . . .

Love is worth living!!!

. . . all else repulses me.

FOUR

BUILDING WITH YOUR HANDS AND YOUR HEART

We all have so very much. *Our cups runneth over.* Maybe not where money is concerned but certainly with our potential. The feeling of love carries a commitment and a responsibility which needs to be honored.

Many people seem to be going through a phase of "seeking themselves." In so doing there is a personal selfishness created either by not sharing that search with others, or by using others as a crutch. There is an attitude of "I won't get too close" because "I am afraid to love since I've already been hurt" or they hold so tight to a relationship they suffocate, or squeeze the life out of it with heavy emotional dependency. Either way, love does not seem to find fertile ground in which to grow.

There are so many kinds of love to which we are answerable. This feeling man calls love is communicated in endless ways. Sometimes it travels as wisdom, sometimes it flows down the cheeks of sorrow, sometimes its vehicle is trust, sometimes the body feels its pleasure. Sometimes it is dressed as hurt, sometimes it builds the new and other times it tears down the old; sometimes love takes the form of teacher while other times it becomes the student.

Devotion is love's greatest asset through all the many different channels. It has the endurance to travel the world, to travel a human lifetime over the roughest terrain and through the most violent of storms. We simply have to learn to appreciate the vehicle on which we are traveling. Learn all its parts, for devotion can be as forever as the celestial bodies that fill the spaces in the universe.

Love is not simply expressed by emotions, sexual desire, shows of affection, caresses of the body, moments of passion, or the sharing of a bed. Can only these kinds of love create motivation and strong foundations enduring the years? Can they outlast the aging body or conflicts of interests which may arise? Can the heart, using emotions predominantly, build a relationship which is fulfilling?

Is love in balance just because we may be living in a house with someone, starting a business to achieve success, learning to make money, pursuing Art for fame, or making friends to further our own interests?

Should not affection be mixed with intelligence; should not sensuality be mixed with knowledge? Hands which explore the body can also create a visual image from the mind.

What delight we take in one another's presence.
Happiness is relived each time we spend moments
together. We take pride in watching each other grow. We
feel contentment when we fulfill each other's needs. We
feel respect toward one another when our learning takes
us up another step to ourselves—to be able just to feel
deeply towards each other. Is not love in its purest form
the sacrificing of our own wants for the necessities of
others?

How can we speak of love when the words are idle chatter, spoken as we would describe a place where we have not been? When we are speaking of love because it is the social thing to do? Love spoken without true feeling lacks substance because it is love without identity! Often the mirror into which we are looking gives back a faceless image.

How can we project love with our hearts as an extension of our hands? How can we project love with our hands as an extension of our hearts? Can our faculties become the tools of our trade, our profession, the stimulation of our spirit, when we were never taught how to use them?

There is intrinsic beauty . . . magnificence . . . undaunted strength . . . in the everlasting and divine goodness that loving bestows on all it touches. I find myself feeling extremely humble in the knowledge of that with which our Creator has endowed us. And I am filled with continual torment that I may not be using these qualities at all times.

How can we feel the deep meaning of affection and sexual expression—the most exalted single flow of all our energies combined—when we don't know how to use our bodies? We don't know our physical form intimately enough nor do we understand the incredible energy it contains.

How can we understand the spectrum of love unless we realize love is not just emotion or sex or fun times or giving material gifts or making money or supporting someone or using someone? Love is collecting feelings instead of things! Love is also a struggle to attain goals, ideals, building a life for oneself or helping others build their lives. It is devotion to people with whom we are involved—and it is hard work; the sweat and toil of one's sowing.

The harder you work at love the more time you spend with love.

How can we build relationships unless we allow ourselves the time, using our hands and our hearts together. Love changes like the cycles of the days and the seasons. The truth of love is the days and the seasons for they always are and always will be. During their cycles there are things that are born, things that grow, things that change, and things that die. All are a part of their reason for existing and human relationships are the same.

Perhaps you ask yourself: "How can I trust my feelings when my emotions have been distorted and abused by others? How can I trust the actions of my body when what I tried to build was either torn down or never completed?" You may reflect: "I sent out positive energy and it came back negative energy. I trusted people's words and found they were lies. I gave consideration and respect and received indifference. I reached out to touch and was repulsed. I gave all that I knew of myself only to have my being used to gratify the wants and desires of others and was then discarded—thrown into the trash barrel of the past."

Pull yourself out of the depths of non-expression and climb the cliffs of perseverance to a higher plateau where your life has brighter meaning.

Our first responsibility is to ourselves. We should
become our own best friend, a true companion, learning
to respect our own acts. We should feel comfortable with
our personality for it follows us as a shadow follows the
sun. We should feel comfortable by exercising our
feelings. We should know we have worth and
importance. To love ourselves is to use our minds to
guide us away from the ordinary, the mediocre—away
from blind acceptance; guiding us to the joy that being
unique creates. This is the balance in any enlightened,
harmonious society, no matter how small, no matter how
large. We should not be intimidated by another man's
reasoning, no matter how important or influential he
may be.

Can we not bridge contrasts and contradictions that make us different through a one-to-one relationship? Can we not give back to people their true natures rather than always trying to change innocent love with logic? Analyze every action, dissect a simple feeling until we are left with only many scattered pieces? Some feelings require neither questions nor answers. When we are able to release this vital force within us, taking off our armor to reveal our true natures, others will feel free to do the same.

I have been given the greatest of gifts by our Creator: to approach life through my body. My senses are aroused by the stimuli of experience, by allowing life to flow *through* me, not just *to* me. When I write these words, my hands become a tool in the building of what my heart feels. We share . . . When I make love to another human being not only my hands but all parts of my body become many tools that can enhance the feeling of the heart. Let us make love, not just sex.

The more I release this vital force, my body, the greater becomes your awareness of me. The body needs the constant giving and receiving of affection to stay healthy.

I have known many people who were richly endowed with sensuality, whose potential for love was incredible. Their fulfillment and joy consisted of being easily aroused by their senses and they were able to give spontaneously of themselves. I have also seen these same people rejected by others who through ignorance and suspicion denied the purity of the love these people expressed.

Many people's bodies are asleep, having gone to sleep as children. There are sleeping children all over the world who are waiting to be awakened to the threshold of their own natural growth and maturity.

Countless numbers of people are stifled by their upbringing, holding tightly to their past, suffocating by their mere existence, feeling inadequate and alone in the use of this most precious of gifts—their body. The body becomes stagnant if the mind doesn't move it and the heart doesn't inspire it.

So construct your relationships with life and people as a builder of love, building with your hands (body) and with your heart (mind)!

It's time to wake up.

Look about!

FIVE

ORIGINAL TRUTH

Early one hot summer day, while buying food supplies in a small town located deep in the redwoods, I found a beautiful Monarch butterfly lying on the asphalt. When I picked him up I saw that his delicate wings were torn and tattered. He was dying, I believe. How long he had been there I don't really know. Such an incredible little creature whose colors and design would make the greatest crown jewels look dull by comparison. He held tight to my finger lest the wind carry him back to the bleakness of the street.

I walked to the edge of town through the trees, to a small meadow by the river, with him on my finger. Placing my hand in the shelter of the tall grass I waited for him to drawl onto the earth floor. He didn't move. Possibly he didn't have the strength—so I nudged him but he held on, as though he had chosen not to leave me. I thought, "Why don't you crawl to the grass where you could die in peacc. If man and his environment have done this cruel thing to you, let go of my finger, for I already feel the shame and guilt that has brought us together." I gently forced him off my finger. As I walked away I was plagued by his unnecessary death.

In the morning before life began to stir I got up and went to where I had left him. He was lying in the very same spot. I reached down and touched him every so lightly but he didn't move. Then I knew life had left this creature. His beautiful wings would never again flutter in the wind nor would children again see this particular miracle of creation.

I watched another butterly from across the meadow as he came toward me flying low over the grass. Maybe he was looking for his friend, for he kept landing on the blades of grass then would search another area. Or maybe he had escaped man's environment, as his friend had not, and was just tired from his flight.

Yesterday, I found another butterfly near a brick wall in the city. She was not as battered as the other but I could see she was very tired from flying through the city corridors. She was lost and could not find her way back to her natural environment. I picked her up carefully and carried her in the palm of my hand to a park. As I walked the wind blew her from my hand and she fell to the ground, trying to move her wings, trying to fly. I placed her back in my hand and continued walking. When I reached the park I put her in a large knothole of a tree so the wind would not carry her back to the cement sidewalks. I felt she would have a better chance to survive.

Many of us are as battered by man's environment as is the butterfly—either physically or mentally. Many look for a route of escape to another place, another way. Like the young men who fled their country because they didn't believe in killing—their consciences could not justify their country's purpose. Like many pilgrims who elect other beliefs to find a better way. This exodus from conformity is taking thousands of people to a more natural environment. We have been indoctrinated to our original sin. Now we are searching for our original innocence . . . original truth.

SIX

THE REBELLION

There is a philosophical rebellion maturing in our country. Recent developments have assisted its growth. Where is this rebellion headed? What kind of revolutionary changes does it purpose? Is an expansion of loving a part of it? Who are the leaders? Who are the followers?

Many people no longer have faith in the words or actions of the men who dictate their futures in many facets of our society. Young people are even questioning their parents' values which they are finding inadequate for their own self-identity. Yet masses of people still continue to accept the dogma which controls their lives. Are they afraid, and if they are, of what are they afraid?

The young people are the most dissatisfied group because the traditional concepts have been largely shattered: family unity, the church, government, sexual ethics, and attitudes toward material wealth. The old traditions are being challenged and the very core of Western culture is weakening. What new foundation is being proposed? What will be built on this new foundation?

The feelings about which I write are derived from the many people with whom I have communicated as I journey the highways of my society. They speak freely about deep-seated problems which concern them, not only on the personal level but also on the social level.

An elderly couple, living in Los Angeles, decided to sell their home of thirty years and move instead into an apartment. They felt at that time there was too much work and responsibility, too great a burden in their old age, in maintaining a house. But recently they changed their minds because social problems, the cost and quality of commercial food, and the insecurity of the economy brought them to the realization that their home was the most secure thing they could have. The large lawn surrounding their house could be utilized to grow food, and since the house was paid for they had only to worry about the exorbitant property taxes each year. Fortunately their son could help them financially or they might otherwise have lost their home, as had many other older couples, due to extreme taxation. They felt that struggle from their own home gave them a better chance of survival as society deteriorated around them.

A young boy of eighteen and his friend decided to move to Alaska where they would work. They intended to buy land on which to live. They'd lost faith in their society and were pessimistic about its future. They gathered food supplies which could be stored without spoiling, and they bought tools and implements that would help them survive in the woods. They had several books on survival in the wilderness. Their decision to emigrate was prompted by their feeling that nuclear war was imminent because people no longer cared about one another.

One young man had accumulated many possessions including a customized Ford van, a stereo, tape deck, motorcycle, many stylish clothes, and he spent a lot of money on entertainment. He seemed never to be fulfilled or happy. After meeting several unique people whose values were different than his (they valued feelings instead of things), he began taking the time to find out why they had chosen their way. He found these people more real than those he had previously thought of as his friends. By their examples they opened him to thinking about new feelings. He longed to experience a new way, not exactly their way but another way of life for himself that would utilize some of their example.

He sold his possessions, took what money he had, and moved to a large lake he had visited several times in the past. With much struggle and determination he began to build a houseboat at the edge of the lake. He lived on the boat as it was being constructed, feeling great pride and self-realization in this new venture.

The simple way of life, the stimulation created by his environment, his excitement at making a decision had showed him a way out of the grasp of materialism. He had always been a part of the waste. He had owned many things he had not needed but wanted only out of habit. Until he'd met his new friends he'd assumed his life was a good one, but with this change in his life he now found he needed far less than what he'd had in the past. There was no longer room for waste.

A girl had been raised by parents who were strictly religious. The parents were part of the affluent society living in one of the better neighborhoods of suburbia. She had accepted that marriage and having children was something expected of her as a woman. Taking care of a home would be her only responsibility; pleasing her husband would be her only joy. But though she did not feel these things she never questioned them openly because her inner self feared to be thought weird or abnormal. So until she left home for a summer of travel, she carried this inner conflict which caused her much pain and suffering. On her travels she met many different types of people, many unlike those with whom she had grown up, many who, rather than condemn her for her feelings intensified her attitude and encouraged her to think for herself.

When she finally got the courage to make her own decision she found she didn't want to marry or have children. She felt there were already too many children in the world that nobody wanted. There were too many young people lost in the interchanges of emotional strife connecting society's structured freeways.

She no longer felt the restrictions that society and her parents had once placed upon her as a female. No longer would she stand in the shadow of any man. She felt her own light. She would now love many people and help to care for the lonely children. Her true nature had emerged into joy and understanding. Now she had choices.

A young married couple (the husband had a good job with a large company) decided to buy a farm, to change their way of life. They felt that pollution, the noise and clutter of the city, were detrimental to them and to the children they hoped to have one day. But land was extremely expensive and they found they couldn't afford to fulfill their dream alone. So they got together with several other young couples who had the same dream, pooled their money and resources, and bought a tract of land where they could live as a small community within a life style of their choosing. Each contributed his or her talents for the benefit of the group. While there would be great struggle in their new existence, their own incentive would be their strongest asset.

These are a few of the many people I have known who have become part of the rebellion that is now surging above the surface of blind acceptance within the structured parent society in which most people live.

Many are calling for change, crying out to the people to get involved in the rebellion, to re-establish their lives with renewed purpose and direction. Spend your money on the rebuilding of families. Bring people back together. Save what is left of the natural earth.

Many new communities of people are springing up all over the country. They are composed mainly of people dissatisfied with the parent society. They are becoming families with a new meaning to that word. The concept of a man, a woman, and children forming an intimate family unit is slowly changing. Many of the new groups of people are now as varied as are the types of human beings. There are communities where two men or two women are accepted as a family, while elsewhere any number of people living together in a home are considered a family. Any combination of human beings who love and care about each other can be a family. As these kinds of communities increase in number they begin to form a parallel society within the parent society. They are still isolated one from another but in time, as more and more are created, they will come together for their own survival, merging their new ways of life, new attitudes, new values as did the pioneers during the birth and initial growth of our country. These are the pioneers of today.

We are consuming enormous quantities of food . . .
products . . . energy; we waste much of what we have
because our appetites come from our wants, our desires,
our lust, our greed, our emotions. Our waste is the result
of gorging ourselves with wants instead of understanding
our needs. Each of us carries this shame and guilt. Look
at the things in our homes: our gadgets, our comforts,
our wardrobes, our vehicles. We speak so often of the
solutions, but we continue to live with the same
problems.

We must, now—not tomorrow, create a balance in our lives between our consumption (what we take from life) and our production (what we give to life) on both the emotional and physical levels. Separation weakens our spirit. Segregation depletes our strength. Lack of awareness will surely destroy our civilization if we continue to close our eyes to this truth. If we are so selfish and ignorant, perhaps we deserve to perish.

Philosophy is the search for truth. I call this a philosophical rebellion. Some people may call it a rebellion for survival.

When tomorrow becomes today, start packing for your new journey. Put your old attitudes to which you no longer relate in the trunk along with those material possessions for which you will no longer have a need. In the suitcase of your mind, leave plenty of room for love. On your journey you will be collecting many new feelings as your soul and dignity expand into a higher consciousness.

SEVEN

THE LETTER

My dear friend;

The cycles of my life came and went as my wrinkles
became more pronounced and the trees grew taller but
fewer. Once in awhile I'd find a stray white hair in my
beard, not yet stained by pollution.

Turmoil continues between countries. Peace is still not as
popular as is war. New inventions keep making life easier
and my people fatter. Science is accelerating at a
fantastic pace, changing our society with its magic while
more artificial stimulants are being found to replace the
simple universal qualities of the individual.

Progress is my people's creed and nature feels the brunt
of our new life, liberty and the pursuit of happiness. Our
government is performing many miracles with welfare
and food stamps and unemployment benefits which too
often become substitutes for human incentive. Poverty of
the mind is massacring healthy human bodies. Our rich
become more influential and our poor become more
abundant. Being stoned on drugs, booze or money is still
the false enlightenment of many.

Our youth inherit what our social order has created. I personally feel we are seducing our young people by not giving them the freedom to be themselves, forcing them to accept our thinking without choice and scaring them into submission by threatening them with God concepts of good and evil. Interpretation of social conduct should come from love—a love so expansive that our imagination cannot fathom any boundaries.

Our Creator was so wise in giving man free choice. Each man must wade through the debris of many thoughts and concepts to find his own original innocence and truth. Nothing is absolute, so all judgments must be flexible to allow the discovery of universal truths for all men and individual truths which create difference. Our people must be able to know (not just think) that each one of us possesses a free spirit.

A government or church can only guide a person's thoughts, suggest ideas of behavior where loving is concerned. I am saddened each time I am told a person is afraid to show me love. It's not that they don't feel love or affection, it's just that somewhere in the past someone in authority taught them to separate loving into categories of right and wrong. God must feel great pain to see man legislate loving. Maybe the raindrops are *really* His tears.

Maybe *your* country, my friend, is a place of tranquility and untouched beauty unfolding majestic mountains, rivers and the coastal regions of *your* land. Maybe *your* cities abound with flowers and trees and acres of clover and grasses, and *your* small buildings reflect the personality of *your* people. Maybe *your* people collect feelings instead of things. Maybe *your* lives are uncomplicated and filled with the richness of love. Maybe I could share *my* life with you, in love, and live out *my* years without suffering or supression; but I'm sorry, my friend, I cannot forsake *my* country. It has helped to make *me* what I am—what you love about *me*. I cannot run away from the boundless energy and potential that lies deep within *my* people.

We are young, have much to learn, and have made many mistakes. We have growing pains, and our greed and money hunger may someday strip us of our creature comforts, power and blind acceptance, showing us instead humility and compassion for difference. We may one day tear down the monuments we built to our inflated egos. The ignorant men who now control our lives may topple from their thrones because we little people will care enough to get involved; to change, to dedicate our lives to the rebuilding of a society built upon all types of love as the reason.

I feel I am still in the promised land, my friend, where love is now beginning to direct our destinies. My choice to stay was made years ago, for this is my home—from the Pacific to the Atlantic—from Canada to Mexico. I was born on her soil and my flesh and bones will go back into her earth, nurturing new growth.

Should she ever fall, her society crumbling and decaying from internal strife, I (and others like me) will find the strength and determination to pick up the scattered pieces, to help rebuild and become a better example for the world.

Thank you for your love, your offers of sharing, and your concern for my happiness and well-being, but I must stay here. Here I will try to construct a better way, to leave my footprints on her history so future generations will know I once lived, bled, suffered, loved and cared enough to fight for a man's free spirit and the beauty of the individual. My people are a part of me and as they hurt so do I. As they live with injustice so do I. As long as the individual nature is repressed by social order, I cannot find personal peace—my soul is linked like a chain to my people's bondage.

How can any man divorce himself from the simple, unrestricted love of his fellow man when we all belong to the same God, to the same family, to the same planet, to the same universe and have the same love within us all?

Must I have a reason to love you; cannot love be my reason?

LOVE IS MY REASON

OTHER BOOKS BY WALTER RINDER

LOVE IS AN ATTITUDE

SPECTRUM OF LOVE

THIS TIME CALLED LIFE

THE HUMANNESS OF YOU, Volume I

THE HUMANNESS OF YOU, Volume II

FOLLOW YOUR HEART

WILL YOU SHARE WITH ME?

CELESTIAL ARTS BOOK LIST

LOVE IS AN ATTITUDE, poetry and photographs by Walter Rinder.
    03-0 Paper @ $3.95   04-9 Cloth @ $7.95

THIS TIME CALLED LIFE, poetry and photographs by Walter Rinder.
    05-7 Paper @ $3.95   06-5 Cloth @ $7.95

SPECTRUM OF LOVE, poetry by Walter Rinder with David Mitchell art.
    19-7 Paper @ $2.95   20-0 Cloth @ $7.95

FOLLOW YOUR HEART, poetry by Walter Rinder with Richard Davis art.
    39-1 Paper @ $2.95

THE HUMANNESS OF YOU, Vol. 1, art and philosophy by Walter Rinder.
    47-2 Paper @ $2.95

THE HUMANNESS OF YOU, Vol. 2, art and philosophy by Walter Rinder.
    54-5 Paper @ $2.95

VISIONS OF YOU, poetry by George Betts and photography by Robert Scales.
    07-3 Paper @ $3.95

MY GIFT TO YOU, poetry by George Betts and photography by Robert Scales.
    15-4 Paper @ $3.95

YOU & I, poetry and photography by Leonard Nimoy.
    26-X Paper @ $3.95   27-8 Cloth @ $7.95

WILL I THINK OF YOU?, poetry and photography by Leonard Nimoy.
    70-7 Paper @ $3.95

SPEAK THEN OF LOVE, poetry by Andrew Oerke with Asian art.
    29-4 Paper @ $3.95

I AM, concepts of awareness in poetic form by Michael Grinder with color art.
    25-1 Paper @ $2.95

GAMES STUDENTS PLAY, transactional analysis in schools by Ken Ernst.
    16-2 Paper @ $3.95   17-0 Cloth @ $7.95

GUIDE FOR SINGLE PARENTS, transactional analysis by Kathryn Hallett.
    55-3 Paper @ $3.95   64-2 Cloth @ $7.95

PASSIONATE MIND, guidance and understanding by Joel Kramer.
    63-4 Paper @ $3.95

SENSIBLE BOOK, understanding children's senses by Barbara Polland.
    53-7 Paper @ $3.95

THIS TIMELESS MOMENT, Aldous Huxley's life by Laura Huxley.
    22-5 Paper @ $4.95

HEALING MIND, explains the healing powers of the mind by Dr. Irving Oyle.
    80-4 Paper @ $4.95

HOW TO BE SOMEBODY, a guide for personal growth by Yetta Bernhard.
    20-9 Paper @ $4.95

CREATIVE SURVIVAL, the problems of single mothers by Persia Woolley.
    17-9 Paper @ $4.95

FAT LIBERATION, the awareness technique to losing weight by Alan Dolit.
    03-9 Paper @ $3.95

ALPHA BRAIN WAVES, explanation of same by D. Boxerman and A. Spilken.
    16-0 Paper @ $4.95

INWARD JOURNEY, art as therapy by Margaret Keyes.
    81-2 Paper @ $4.95

GOD, poetic visions of the abstract by Alan Watts.
    75-8 Paper @ $3.95

Write for a free catalog to:
CELESTIAL ARTS   231 Adrian Road   Millbrae, California 94030